You Don't Frighten Me!

When I get frightened:

I stack,
I pack,
I pile,
I file
all my teddies around my bed.
And like soldiers at attention
they offer me a wall of protection.

Then I skip into my bed.
squeeze deep down into my duvet
and whisper,
"Come on Darkness,
you big, black, bullying,
bubble of trouble.
I'm ready with my teddies
and you don't frighten me!"

Ian Souter

Other fantastic poetry collections
from Scholastic:

Animal Poems
Dinosaur Poems
Disgusting Poems
Family Poems
Funny Poems
Magic Poems
Pet Poems
School Poems
Silly Poems

SPOOKY POEMS

Compiled by Jennifer Curry
Illustrated by Woody Fox

SCHOLASTIC

This book is for my granddaughter,
LAURA CURRY, who likes to be frightened...
but only a little bit!

Published by Scholastic Ltd,
Book End, Range Road, Witney,
Oxfordshire OX29 0YD
www.scholastic.co.uk
Designed using Adobe InDesign

Compiled by Jennifer Curry
Internal illustrations by Woody Fox
Cover illustration by Tony De Saulles

Printed in Great Britain by CPI Group (UK) Ltd, Croydon, CR0 4YY
© 2015 Scholastic Ltd
1 2 3 4 5 6 7 8 9 5 6 7 8 9 0 1 2 3 4

British Library Cataloguing-in-Publication Data
A catalogue record for this book is available from the British Library.

ISBN 978-1407-15890-7

CONTENTS

WHO LIVES IN THIS HAUNTED HOUSE?

NOTHING THERE AT ALL

A GREAT HUGE HORRIBLE HORRIBLE

EYES ARE DARK AS HOLLY

BAG OF BONES

MAD-AND-MONSTERED DARKNESS

PLUCKER OF MOONBEAMS

LAST WORD

FIRST WORD

The Haunted Poem

This poem is haunted by a ghost.
No one has ever seen him
but every single person who reads this poem
will be left in no doubt of his existence.

Sometimes he changes the order of words the,
mixes the lettwfsahj4el8r7fn666 pu
or even makes them

You'll be halfway through the **BOO!**
verse and he'll interrupt and make you jump.

Whole sections are **WOOHOOO**o filled
with his **WOO** spooky moaning and groaning
then suddenly fade away.

Occasionally   will be hidden
in the   of the page.

At any time he may frighten you
or add rude words when you're not bum
expecting it
so that when knickerscheesytoes you read them
you blush and go bright GOTCHA! red.

HAHAHAHAAA!
His laughter will echo in your brain
HAHAHAHAAA!
and ring constantly ring constantly ring ring
constantly
HAHAHAHAAA!
in your ears
HAHAHAHAAA!

Even now he is watching your every move
as you read the haunted poem…
every twitch, every blink, every sigh, every
glance,
so that just when you think you've read the last
word
and the poem is over he leaves a ghostly
message,
just for you…
WATCH OUT BEHIND YOU…

Paul Cookson

TERRIBLE TOAST AND FROZEN LOLLIES

Morning Monster

(or The Breakfast Break-Out)

At breakfast this morning
when I cracked my egg,
a monster jumped out
with a hairy leg.
I'm telling you straight
(and it ain't no joke)
he was small and fierce
and covered in yolk.

Well, he stood quite still
and he looked at me.
Then he washed himself
in my cup of tea.
He dried himself
with the morning post,
then he helped himself
to my piece of toast.

Tony Mitton

Weighty Problem

A ghost used to spook about Pinner,
Haunting the place for some dinner,
He needed some weight,
But whatever he ate,
He got thinner and thinner and thinner…

Jenni Sinclair

Vanilla Van Ghost

The path to the house was darkened
As shadows fell here and there.
The owl was blindly hooting
And the moon had a wild-eyed stare.

Over the roof-tops hurtled –
As I walked towards my door –
The shape of a ghostly ice-cream van
Which chilled me to the core.

It few right down beside me,
As soft as a giant bat.
The window opened silently
And an ice-cream landed – *SPLAT!*

In fear I turned and stumbled
Headlong towards my door
But the ghostly van pursued me
And a demon voice cried – *MORE!*

A rain of frozen lollies
Came showering on my head
In a range of creepy colours –
Spooky White to Vampire Red!

I leaped through my open door
And shut it with a – *SNICK!*
But a choc-ice whizzed through the letter-box
And the demon voice yelled – *LICK!*

Thank goodness when I woke
I found it was just a dream –
A dream of *Vanilla Van Ghost*
The demon seller of ice-cream!

Ivan Jones

Terrible Toast

"This toast," moaned the ghost
"is impossible to chew.
The trouble is, my teeth
just float right through."

"Allow me," smiled the vampire,
with a grin of delight.
"I'll show you how it's done.
You watch. I'll bite."

So the vampire ate the lot,
but what he liked most
was the red, sticky jam
which he licked from the toast.

Tony Mitton

Midnight in the Chip Shop

At midnight in the chip shop
The door of the freezer creaks slowly open
And the inmates slither out

The cod cackles
The salmon simpers
And the haddock howls at the moon

The pickled onions unpickle their brains
  and scream
And the battered sausage batters a saveloy
  into submission

A light shines at the window
Hello, hello, hello
Says a deep round voice
Something fishy going on in there

Graeme Curry

Gobbledespook

Can you read this message?

The bottom of each letter

was bitten off and gobbled

by a ghost who knew no better.

Gina Douthwaite

SPOOKING AROUND IN SCHOOLS

Watch Your Teacher Carefully

It happened in school last week
when everything seemed fine
assembly, break, science and spelling
three twelves are four times nine.

But then I noticed my teacher
scratching the skin from her cheek
a forked tongue flicked from her lips
her nose hooked into a beak.

Her twenty arms grew longer
they ended in terrible claws
by now she was orange and yellow and green
with crunching great teeth in her jaws.

Her twenty eyes were upon me
as I ran from the room for the Head
got to his office, burst through the door
met a bloodsucking alien instead.

Somehow I got to the staffroom
the doorknob was dripping with slime
inside were seven hideous things
who thought I was dinner-time.

I made my escape through a window
just then a roaring sound
knocked me over flat on my face
as the whole school left the ground.

Powerful rockets pushed it
back into darkest space
all I have left are the nightmares
and these feathers that grow on my face.

David Harmer

Sam Spook

(the curse of all teachers)

Sammy was a teacher-spook
and he spooked around in schools
spooking out for teachers
in class
     at desks
          on stools…
He'd wriggle up their trouser legs
he'd make them jump and squeal
and turn them into funny things
like mud
      or orange peel.

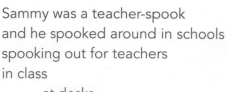

He'd turn them into awful things
cabbages and flies
bits of string and paper
bits of chewed-up pies!
Miss Thompson was a sausage
Miss Cummins was a clock
Miss Angel was a plug-hole
Miss Ryan was a sock!

He'd turn them into ANYTHING
– so be careful where you tread –
that custard could be teacher…
and that apple core –
                    The Head!

Peter Dixon

Quieter Than Snow

I went to school a day too soon
And couldn't understand
Why silence hung in the yard like sheets
Nothing to flap or spin, no creaks
or shocks of voices, only air.

And the car park empty of teachers' cars
Only the first September leaves
Dropping like paper.
No racks of bikes
No kicking legs, no fights,
No voices, laughter, anything.

Yet the door was open.
My feet sucked down the corridor.
My reflection walked with me past the hall.
My classroom smelt of nothing

And the silence rolled like thunder in my ears.
At every desk a still child stared at me
Teachers walked through walls and back again
Cupboard doors swung open, and out crept

More silent children, and still more.
They tiptoed round me
Touched me with ice-cold hands
And opened up their mouths with laughter
That was
Quieter than snow.

Berlie Doherty

The Ghoul School Bus

The ghoul school bus
is picking up its cargo
of little horrors.

They must all be home
before first light, when today
turns into tomorrow.

All the sons and daughters of vampires,
little Igors and junior Fangs,
the teenage ghouls with their ghoulfriends
all wail, as the bus bell clangs.

And the driver doesn't look well,
he's robed completely in black,
and the signboard says – *Transylvania,
by way of hell and back.*

The seats are slimy and wet,
there's a terrible graveyard smell,
all the small ghouls cackle and spit,
and practise their ghoulish spells.

The witches are reading their ABCs,
cackling over "D" for disease,
while tomboy zombies are falling apart
and werewolves are checking for fleas.

When the bus slows down to drop them off
at Coffin Corner or Cemetery Gates,
their *mummies* are waiting to greet them
with eyes full of anguish and hate.

The ghoul school bus
is dropping off its cargo
of little horrors.

They must all be home
before first light, when today
turns into tomorrow.

Brian Moses

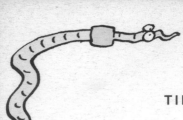

A Schoolgirl Called Julia

There was a young schoolgirl called Julia
whose habits were really peculia!
She'd turn into a bug
or a fat, green-eyed slug,
And giggle, "I knew that would fool ya!"

Jenny Craig

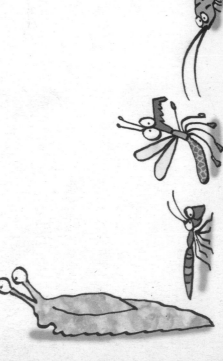

COOL GHOULS

Duppy Dan

Duppy Dan
ain't no livin man

Duppy Dan
done dead an gone

Duppy Dan
nah have foot

Duppy Dan
nah have hand

Yet Duppy Dan cross water
Duppy Dan cross land

Duppy Dan ride white horse
pon pitch dark night

Run like-a-hell stranger
when Duppy Dan tell you goodnight

John Agard

Duppy: A Jamaican word for ghost

House Ghosts

Airing cupboard ghosts
hold music practices
inside the water tank.

Television ghosts
poke crooked fingers
across your favourite programme.

Chimney ghosts
sing one-note songs
over and over in owly voices.

Vacuum-cleaner ghosts
roar and the dust obeys them,
into the bag.

But the worst ghost
Hides under your bed at night.

He makes no noise at all.

Irene Rawnsley

Hallowe'en

Tonight, ghosts climb out of bed,
Tipping the earth from their ears,
Sluggish at first. But then
They whizz round the churchyard,
Dive through each other,
Glow green all over. Some
Take off their heads to
Play football. Others hurdle
Gravestones, or skip with their chains.

Many enjoy a good moan
All night. They drink
Moonbeam cocktails, eat
Barbecued bats with lacings
Of cobweb. They flap away
To yowl on the tiles like
Next door's cat, swing
From the washing-line pretending
To be shirts, dive-bomb
The dog as it whimpers in the kitchen.
Just before dawn, they
Wave to their friends, say
"See you next year," and
Slide back home.

Daphne Schiller

The New Girl

The new girl stood at Miss Moon's desk,
Her face pale as a drawing
On white paper,
Her lips coloured too heavily
With a too-dark crayon.

When the others shouted. "Me! Me!"
I curled my fists,
Tried not to think of friendship,
Or whispered secrets,
Or games for two players.
But the empty seat beside me
Shimmered with need
And my loneliness dragged her like a magnet.

As she sat down
I caught the musty smell of old forests,
Noticed the threads that dangled
At her thin wrists,
The purple stitches that circled
Her swan's neck.
Yet I loved her quietness,
The way she held her pencil
Like a feather,
The swooping curves of her name,
The dreaminess of her cold eyes.

At night, I still wonder
Where she sleeps,
If she sleeps,
And what Miss Moon will say
To her tattered parents
On Open Day.

Clare Bevan

Teeny Tiny Ghost

A teeny, tiny ghost
no bigger than a mouse
at most,
lived in a great big house.

It's hard to haunt
a great big house
when you're a teeny, tiny ghost
no bigger than a mouse
at most.

He did what he could do.

So every dark and stormy night
the kind that shakes the house with fright
if you stood still and listened right,
you'd hear a
teeny
tiny
BOO!

Lilian Moore

My Cat's Ghost

There **are** cat ghosts.

Once, I had a ginger and white cat
who used to wake me with his whiskers
and jump for butterflies
in the summer sun.
Now he is dead –
but sometimes I still see him,
out of the corner of my eye,
my ginger and white cat
ghosting around doorways,
like a memory.

Tim Pointon

Invite to Cool Ghouls

The ghouls would like to invite you
to a party next Saturday week.
Invitations are only extended
to the very best ghouls, the real freaks.

It will be the ghoul bash of the century
the party of parties for sure
so you must do your best
be the gruesomest guest
or you may not get in at the door.

All hair must be horribly spiky
ice-blue or a silvery white.
Dress must be tatty
(*nothing* that's natty)
and the odd touch of spit is all right.

Green teeth will be specially welcome
and in case it slips anyone's mind
foul breath sprays will be
in the washrooms for free
and the slimiest soap you could find.

Oh, and do wear your ghastliest make-up
and practise your wailing and groans
for the highlight's a prize
for the grizzliest smile
and the chilliest, thrilliest moans.

We cannot imagine you'd miss it
but if you *have* to decline
send a first-class reply by bat post saying why
– or don't look for an invite next time!

Patricia Leighton

Ghost-Child

Please Ma, can I
    race on the dodgems,
    ride the big wheel…?

Here comes the train now,
just keep up those moans!
Dangle this cobweb
and rattle those bones!

Please let me out
    for the coconut shy?
    A quick donkey ride?
    Just a look at the sky?

I hear the next train –
remember those groans!
Wave that white sheet please
and rattle those bones!

It's damp and it's dark here –
    I want to get out!
    The carousel's turning,
    I hear the kids shout!

Your job is right here –
now on with those moans!
Just quiver and shiver
and rattle those bones!

Judith Nicholls

A Shy Ghost Called Freddy

There once was a shy ghost called Freddy
Who tried to be brave, bold and steady.
He wailed and he moaned,
He rattled and groaned,
But he'd *rather* stay home with his teddy.

Jenny Craig

WHO LIVES IN THIS HAUNTED HOUSE?

The Jelly Bone Man

The jelly bone man
oozes through the cracks.
Folds himself up
and disappears
into his own hollow heart.
When he comes
to wrap you in a hug,
the sleeves of his coat,
lapels of his jacket,
flap around you –
swallow you up
in a great gulp gulf.

Then he'll spin around
spin...spin – like a terrible top,
until his arms are empty
and his smile is wide open
and his eyes gleam cold as space.
And you?
You'll be gone.
Gone...
Gone...
Into the nothing
the dizzy dark nothing
of the jelly bone...

        ...jelly bone man.

Jan Dean

Holiday Home

This is Sophie's house.
She hides out of sight
in the headless doll
by the sand-pit, in
an egg-cup, a blue mug
with her name on.

She smiles from behind
the toy box, not minding
that the boy picks up
a bear by the leg. Her
eyes are animal eyes in
pictures on the wall.

The boy baths in Sophie's
bath, eats from her dish.
For a special treat he
sits on Sophie's little
red chair, possessing it
as if it were his own.

Sophie is everywhere,
rings from the bell,
sings from the birds
above the bed, but
she and the boy never
meet. Come Saturday

he says goodbye to
Sophie's house, to the
apple trees, to cows
by the fence. Will he
leave some ghost behind
for Sophie to find?

Moira Andrew

I'd Rather Not Tell

Over the bridge
Across the field
up the hill
and down the lane
there's a house in a garden
I visited once
And I'll never go there again.

A house in a garden,
A room in a house,
A box in a room
Where only the mice
Are awake when
– Now and again –
the lid gently opens
All by itself,
And out comes – well?
No, I'd rather not tell.

Over the bridge
Across the field
up the hill
and down the lane
there's a house in a garden
I visited once
And I'll never go there again.

David Orme

The Oak Chest

Darkness. Can you see anything?
The room feels empty now.
Wait. There's a great oak chest
in the corner. You saw it

yesterday, late. Come on. Your hand.
Feel these carvings. A forest, a king
lying under trees, an arrow,
remember? A shield, a date.

And inside? Shall we open it?

I said, Shall we open it?

Fred Sedgwick

Deserted House

Bare branch
taps against broken glass.
A door creaks.
Window sways in the wind.

Listen!

Moonlight
creeps down dark walls.
A tile falls.
Owl waits, silently.

Watch!

Icy wind
stings your cheeks.
A twig scratches.
Cobwebs brush your hand.

Feel

> *...and RUN!*

Judith Nicholls

In the Castle of Gloom

Oh,
it's cold,
it's as cold as a tomb,
and
it's dark
as a windowless room
in
the Castle
the Castle of Gloom.

(Meet your doom......)

No sun through the shutters.
No candle flame gutters.
No log embers glimmer.
No silver plates shimmer.
    No lamps in the hall.
      No brands on the wall.
        No moonbeams at night.
          No starshine.
            No light.

Oh,
it's cold,
it's as cold as a tomb,
and
it's dark
as a windowless room
in
the Castle,
the Castle of Gloom.

(Meet your dooooooooom......)

Wes Magee

Do Not Feed

Ogres are generally
ugly, unfriendly
and huge; especially
fond of the flesh
of a human or two
or three for tea.

Should not be annoyed.
Best to avoid.

Jill Townsend

The Ghost Outside

When I was young I used to live
in a house in a seaside town,
a terraced house on the top of a hill,
two rooms upstairs, three down.

It was a very comfortable home,
of mod cons it had but a few,
and the room I will always remember the most
is the outside one, the Loo.

This unusual little convenience,
the room that was used the most,
was light in the day and dark at night
and inhabited by a ghost.

If careful you could keep yourself safe
if you left, when you'd finished, in a rush;
the trick was to get back into the house
before it completed its flush.

But if you should dally, and hang around
after pulling the chain, in that loo,
you wouldn't have an earthly chance
for the ghost would surely get you.

So on a warm, late summer's eve
when the ghost awoke for the night,
if you had to go, then you had to go,
but you went in a state of fright.

So steady, hand upon the chain,
like a sprinter at the start of a race,
get ready, pull – now run like mad
into the house and…safe.

Robin Mellor

Yesterday Upon the Stair

Yesterday upon the stair
I met a man who wasn't there;
He wasn't there again today,
I wish, I wish he'd go away.

Anon

NOTHING THERE AT ALL

Ghost Hunt

Long after midnight
I searched for the haunted house,
but I didn't see
a speck of a spectre,
nor a fraction of a phantom,
nor a spot of a spook,
nor a pinch of a poltergeist.
I didn't even catch
the sweet scent of a skelington's wellingtons!

Long after midnight
I searched for the haunted house,
but when I couldn't find it
– I gave up the ghost.

John Rice

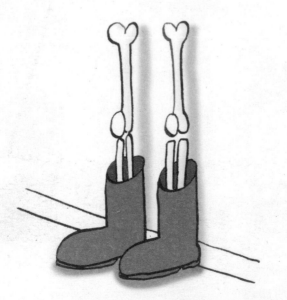

Someone

Someone came knocking
At my wee, small door;
Someone came knocking,
I'm sure – sure – sure;
I listened, I opened,
I looked to left and right,
But nought there was a-stirring
In the still dark night;
Only the busy beetle
Tap-tapping in the wall,
Only from the forest
The screech-owl's call,
Only the cricket whistling
While the dewdrops fall,
So I know not who came knocking,
At all, at all, at all.

Walter de la Mare

Beware

A
ghost is;
a white shadow, in
the darkness, two inky
pools, of nowhere, staring,
a toothless mouth gaping
wide with groaning,
mournful cries,
and chains of
whispers
clanking.
A
ghost is; two arms   suspended, floating,
a body drifting through an old brick wall,
the chill that fills the air when
nothing's there at all,
but echoes,
echoes, softly
tapping.
A ghost is;
the whispering
of the wind,
footsteps
upon the
stairs, as
if some-
thing's
there,
just
barely
seen,
hardly
heard,
not
believed,
but oh,
not quite
dis-
appearing.

David Poulter

Ghost in the Garden

The ghost in the garden
Cracks twigs as she treads
Shuffles the leaves
But isn't there

The ghost in the garden
Snaps back the brambles
So they spring against my legs
But isn't there

Draws spiders' webs across my face
Breathes mist on my cheek
Whispers with bird-breath down my ear
But isn't there

Tosses raindrops down from branches
Splashes the pond
Traces a face in it
That isn't mine

Moves shadows underneath the trees
Too tall, too thin, too tiny to be me
Spreads bindweed out to catch me
Flutters wild wings about my head
Tugs at my hair

But isn't there

And when I look
There's only the bend of grass
Where her running feet
Have smudged the dew
And there's only the sigh
Of her laughter
Trickling
Like
Moonlight
On
Wet
Weeds.

Berlie Doherty

Ghosts

That's right. Sit down and talk to me.
What do you want to talk about?

Ghosts. You were saying that you believe
in them.
Yes, they exist, without a doubt.

What, bony white nightmares that rattle
and glow?
No, just spirits that come and go.

I've never heard such a load of rubbish.
Never mind, one day you'll know.

What makes you so sure?

I said:
What makes you so sure?

Hey,
Where did you go?

Kit Wright

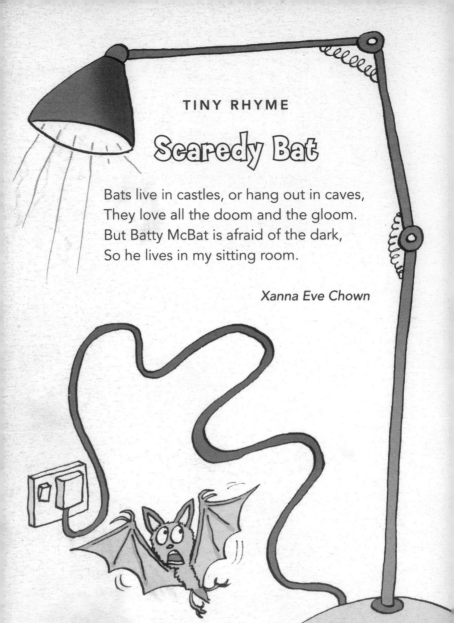

Scaredy Bat

Bats live in castles, or hang out in caves,
They love all the doom and the gloom.
But Batty McBat is afraid of the dark,
So he lives in my sitting room.

Xanna Eve Chown

A GREAT HUGE HORRIBLE HORRIBLE

It

It was huge,
It was enormous,
It came dripping from the sea;
It wobbled down the promenade,
It passed quite close to me!
It ruined all the flower-beds,
It upset an ice-cream stall,
It was like a giant jellyfish and
It had no eyes at all.
It cleared the paddling-pool of kids,
Its feelers swung and swayed,

It seemed to like the fruit machines as
It oozed through the arcade.
It burst the turnstile on the pier as
It squeezed its grey mass through,
It left a horrid track behind –
It was like a trail of glue.
It reached the pier's end railings and
It forced them till they split.
It flopped back down into the sea and
It vanished. That was **It**.

Eric Finney

Scary Night

On Hallowe'en night, as she smoothed my
   bedspread,
My mum saw me shivering, and here's what she said:
"Forget all those stories you've heard and
   you've read.
Now, why don't you lie down and sleep tight instead?
No creatures'll get you. You've nothing to dread."
My dad stood beside her and nodded his head…
And so did the witch as she flew overhead
And so did the monster from under my bed
And so did the werewolf who looked underfed
And so did the zombie, although kind of dead
And so did our neighbours, as each of them fled
And so did the vampire, as his victim bled
And so did his victim whose neck was all red
And me, I just shivered beneath my bedspread
And thought of the stories I'd heard and I'd read.

Nick Toczek

The Relentless Pursuit of the 12-Toed Snortiblog!

It SNIFFs you out: "sffft, sfft, sffft"
It HEARS your heartbeat: "dup dup dup"
It SEES your terror: "aaaaaah!"
It TASTES revenge: "mmmmmmmmmmm"

It will grab you with all twelve toes…

It will give you a big kiss:

"SHSPPLUKKLSSMLOOPSCHPPWASSSSHLAKKK"!

Anon

Killer Carrots

They arose from the earth,
Tall and thin,
They had no eyes,
Yet I could feel their cold stare upon me.
They had no mouths
Yet I could hear their voices ringing in my ears.
In armies of twenty, thirty, forty,
They troop into towns and cities,
People are screaming.

And shouting for help.
But the carrots storm on and on.
No one can stop them as they go marching on.
All over the land,
All over the sea,
The whole world's in their power,
Soon we shall be
Slaves kneeling at their roots.

Abigail Troop (aged 11)

Just Pretending

Hey Mum, look out!
There's a monster on our path.
Guess what, Mum?
He splashed me,
playing dolphins in the bath.

That fooled you, Mum!

Listen Mum, that monster's
knocking at the door.
Honest Mum, it wasn't me
made muddy marks
across the kitchen floor.

Just kidding, Mum!

Take care, Mum
the monster's on the roof.
Oh no, he's not, he's
watching us. Honest Mum,
I'm telling you the truth!

Tricked you again, Mum!

Quick Mum, the monster's
jumping the garden gate!
Hey Mum, he's chasing you!
Watch out, Mum – I'm not
pretending! Oh dear, too late!

AAAAAAAAAAArgh!

I warned you, Mum!

Moira Andrew

House for Sale

It's one thing to find monsters
on the mountain top, head in
the clouds, feet tucked
under a duvet of heather.

It's okay for them to take up
residence beneath the ocean
with coral for a pillow, swaying
seaweed their bubbling quilt.

It's perfectly acceptable for
them to live in dark damp caves
where bats sing shrill lullabies
and moss makes a luxurious bed.

But when monsters come to buy
the house next door, then it's
something else! You'll trip over
their tails on the garden path.

They'll sleep with smelly feet
stuck out of the window, snore
like volcanos – and if they should
sneeze, then you'll find yourself

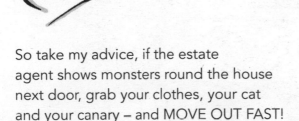

So take my advice, if the estate
agent shows monsters round the house
next door, grab your clothes, your cat
and your canary – and MOVE OUT FAST!

Moira Andrew

The Horny-Galoch

The horny-goloch is an awesome beast,
Soople an' scaly;
It has two horns, an' a hantle o' feet,
An' a forkie tailie.

Anon

EYES ARE DARK AS HOLLY

Green Man in the Garden

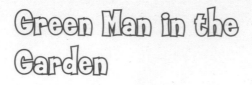

Green man in the garden
  Staring from the tree,
Why do you look so long and hard
  Through the pane at me?

Your eyes are dark as holly,
  Of sycamore your horns,
Your bones are made of elder-branch,
  Your teeth are made of thorns.

Your hat is made of ivy-leaf,
  Of bark your dancing shoes,
And evergreen and green and green
  Your jacket and shirt and trews.

Leave your house and leave your land
  And throw away the key,
And never look behind, he creaked,
  And come and live with me.

I bolted up the window,
  I bolted up the door,
I drew the blind that I should find
  The green man never more.

But when I softly turned the stair
  As I went up to bed,
I saw the green man standing there.
  Sleep well, my friend, he said.

Charles Causley

The Demon-Tree

When I was young
there was a tree…
Oh, how it used to frighten me.

It rose up, huge and fierce,
out of the flat Suffolk fields
and if I saw it in the distance
my heart would leap into my throat.
I'd hurry by, eyes down, hoping
that the ugly, gnarled demon-tree,
with outstretched claws,
would not catch me!

But one wild, windy night
I'd stayed too long at school, was late,
hurrying home across the fields,
driven back by lashing rain and razor-winds,
I found myself huddled under that tree
feeling its strong brown arms protecting me:
daring the rain to make me wet –
the wind to whistle through.
They kept their distance.

Its twisted trunk and knotted limbs
kept me safe and warm
until Dad found me
and took me home.

Jo Vernillo

The Gribble

In the woods the Gribble lives,
he hides behind the trees;
no one ever sees him, but
at night he comes to visit me.

The Gribble tells me stories
of the woods and wind and trees,
and how the leaves dance nightly
to the tune of a moonlit breeze.

He has a face of green and brown
and hands with skin like bark,
he creeps up to my window,
when my room is dark.

I always fall asleep before
the Gribble leaves my room,
but when I wake in the morning
I know he'll come back soon.

In the woods the Gribble lives,
he hides behind the trees;
no one ever sees him, but
at night he comes to visit me.

Robin Mellor

Trees

The trees are shrieking
Their hands thrust up in fright
Like an army of bone-men on the hill
Stopped in their tracks and turned to skin
  and stone.

Berlie Doherty

The Two Old Women of Mumbling Hill

The two old trees on Mumbling Hill,
They whisper and chatter and never keep still.
What do they say as they lean together
In rain or sunshine or windy weather?

There were two old women lived near the hill,
And they used to gossip as women will
Of friends and neighbours, houses and shops,
Weather and trouble and clothes and crops.

Then one sad winter they both took ill,
The two old women of Mumbling Hill.
They were bent and feeble and wasted away
And both of them died on the selfsame day.

Now the ghosts of the women of Mumbling Hill,
They started to call out loud and shrill,
"Where are the tales we used to tell,
And where is the talking we loved so well?"

Side by side stood the ghosts until
They both took root on Mumbling Hill;
And they turned to trees, and they slowly grew,
Summer and winter the long years through.

In the winter the bare boughs creaked and cried,
In summer the green leaves whispered and sighed;
And still they talk of fine and rain,
Storm and sunshine, comfort and pain.

The two old trees of Mumbling Hill,
They whisper and chatter and never keep still.
What do they say as they lean together
In rain or sunshine or windy weather?

James Reeves

TINY RHYME

Green Man

Green man in the tree
Your midnight eyes gleam out at me.
A robin nests within your crown,
Breast blood red, in branches brown.

Anon

BAG OF
BONES

Old Bill Bones

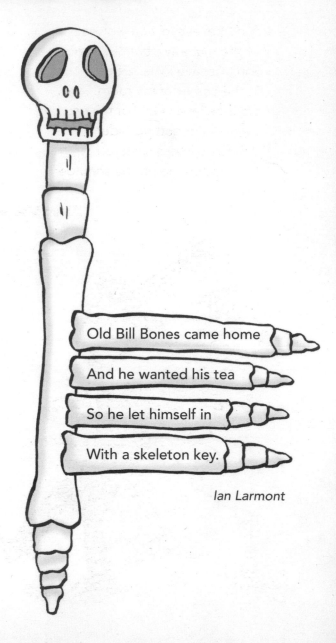

Old Bill Bones came home

And he wanted his tea

So he let himself in

With a skeleton key.

Ian Larmont

Disbelief

I don't believe in werewolves
　　or the mummy from the tomb,
I don't believe in vampires
　　in the corner of my room.
I don't believe in lots of things
　　for now I'm getting older,
But I *do* believe a skeleton
　　just tapped me on the shoulder.

Doug MacLeod

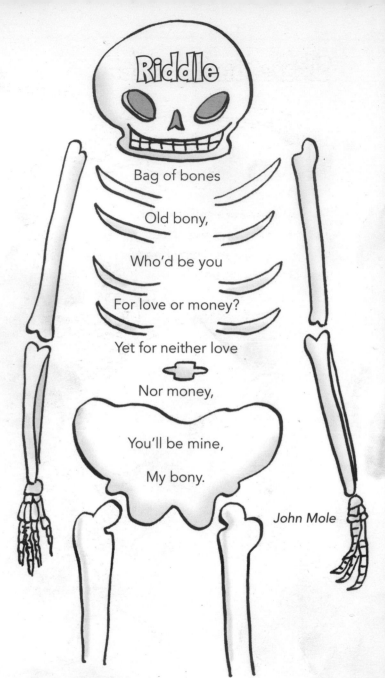

Riddle

Bag of bones

Old bony,

Who'd be you

For love or money?

Yet for neither love

Nor money,

You'll be mine,

My bony.

John Mole

Answer: A skeleton!

Skeleton Parade

The skeletons are out tonight,
They march about the street
With bony bodies, bony heads
And bony hands and feet.

Bony bony bony bones
With nothing in between
Up and down and all around
They march on Hallowe'en.

Jack Prelutsky

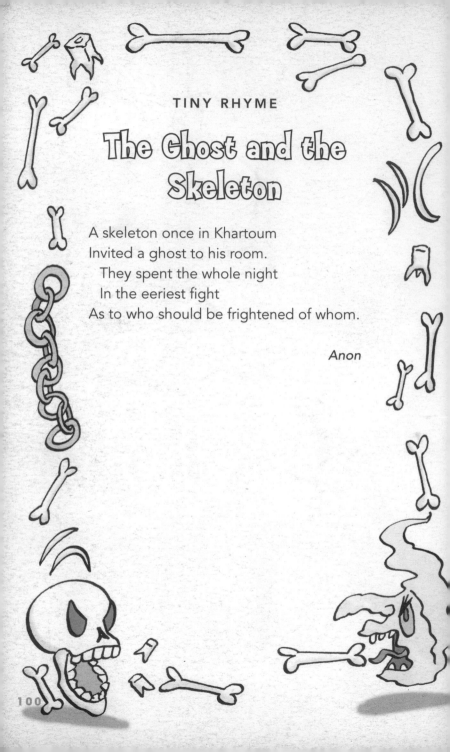

TINY RHYME

The Ghost and the Skeleton

A skeleton once in Khartoum
Invited a ghost to his room.
  They spent the whole night
  In the eeriest fight
As to who should be frightened of whom.

Anon

MAD-AND-
MONSTERED
DARKNESS

The Longest Journey in the World

"Last one in bed
has to switch out the light."
It's just the same every night.
There's a race.
I'm ripping off my trousers and shirt,
he's kicking off his shoes and socks.

"My sleeve's stuck."
"This button's too big for its button-hole."
"Have you hidden my pyjamas?"
"Keep your hands off mine."

If you win
you get where it's safe
before the darkness comes –
but if you lose
if you're last
you know what you've got coming up is
    the journey from the light switch to your bed.
It's the Longest Journey in the World.

"You're last tonight," my brother says.
And he's right.

There is nowhere so dark
as that room in the moment
after I've switched out the light.

There is nowhere so full of dangerous things,
things that love dark places,
things that breathe only when you breathe
and hold their breath when I hold mine.

So I have to say:
"I'm not scared."
That face, grinning in the pattern on the wall,
isn't a face –
"I'm not scared."
That prickle on the back of my neck
is only the label on my pyjama jacket –
"I'm not scared."
That moaning-moaning is nothing
but water in a pipe –
"I'm not scared."

Everything's going to be just fine
as soon as I get into that bed of mine.
Such a terrible shame
it's always the same
it takes so long
it takes so long
it takes so long
to get there.

From the light switch
to my bed
it's the Longest Journey in the World.

Michael Rosen

Time for Bed

Put awa' your book
Turn off the light
Day is düne
Night has begun

Let me tuck you in
All snug and tight
Dream awa' my bairn
Night's just begun

It's a' dark ootside
There's nae stern light
Everyone's quiet
Noo night's begun

I close tight my een
Hide under my covers
Feart to mak' a sound
Syne night's begun

That frichtsome monster
Under ma bed
Is haein' a braw time
Now night's begun

There's mair than one
O' them eldritch sights
Hauntin' ma room
Syne night's begun

They're ahint my curtains
Dancin' on my wa's
Oot they a' come
Now night's begun

I pray to God
Ilka night
To send them awa'
When night's begun

But they willnae go
Wi'oot a fight
So ah'll just hae to wait
Til' morning light

Donna Drever (aged 14)

Night Water

I'm scared at night
when thirst awakes me
and I take me
shaky
through the mad-and-monstered darkness
to the sink.
The fear is with me
as I stoop to stop
the stream of water
with my trembling-tendrilled palm
and take a drink.
I know the ghost
is waiting on
the landing or behind the door
to run his chilly finger
down my spine.
When Mum calls out
"Are you all right?"
I jump out of my skin, then run
to her room so she'll take me
back to mine.

Linda Lee Welch

What's That Down There?

What's that down there?
What's that moving?
What's that moving down
in the dark?
Is it the monster
Who roars
And kills?
Or is it the skeleton
Who rattles his bones?
What's that down there?
What's that moving?
What's that moving down
in the dark?
Is it a bat
Flying through the air?
What's that
in the dark?

Jonathan Matthews (aged 7)

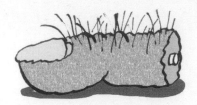

The Hairy Toe

Once there was a woman went out to pick
  beans,
and she found a Hairy Toe.
She took the Hairy Toe home with her,
and that night, when she went to bed,
the wind began to moan and groan.
Away off in the distance
she seemed to hear a voice crying,
"Who's got my Hair-r-ry To-o-oe?
Who's got my Hair-r-ry To-o-oe?"

The woman scrooched down,
'way down under the covers,

and about that time
the wind appeared to hit the house,
smoosh,
and the old house creaked and cracked
like something was trying to get in.
The voice had come nearer,
almost at the door now,
and it said,
"Where's my Hair-r-ry To-o-oe?
Who's got my Hair-r-ry To-o-oe?"

The woman scrooched further down
under the covers
and pulled them tight around her head.
The wind growled around the house
like some big animal
and r-r-um-mbled
over the chimbley.
All at once she heard the door cr-r-a-ack
and Something slipped in
and began to creep over the floor.
The floor went
cre-e-eak, cre-e-eak
at every step that thing took towards her bed.
The woman could almost feel
it bending over her bed.
Then in an awful voice it said:
"Where's my Hair-r-ry To-o-oe?
Who's got my Hair-r-ry To-o-oe?
You've got it!"

Anon
(Traditional American)

from... Duppy Jamboree

"Back to back, belly to belly
Ah don't care at all
For me done dead a'ready.
Back to back, belly to belly
In de duppy jamboree."

What that noise me hearing
Coming from out o' doah?
Mi get out o' bed, pull back de curtain
An peep out tru de window.

Me rub me yeye an look again,
Can't believe wha me just see,
Twenty-seven duppy dere
Staring back at me!

De Devil out deh with dem
With him cow-foot an him horn,
Him long tail wrap right roun him wais'
Him pitchfork in him han.

Lawd, him looking up at me!
Him see me! Him a grin!
It look like sey him come
To punish me for all me sin.

Dem comin to de doorway,
Me noh ready yet fe dead!
Me fly into me mama room
An jump into her bed.

Yeye-water runnin dung me face
Till me can hardly see,
"De duppy dem out o' doah, Mama
Doan mek dem come ketch me!"

Mama hold me tight an laugh,
"Noh mek dem frighten you,
Is not a duppy jamboree,
Is just de Jonkunnu."

Valerie Bloom

*Jonkunnu: As part of the Christmas celebrations in Jamaica,
dancers and musicians put on masks of the characters in
folktales and parade around the streets. The masqueraders
pretend to threaten onlookers who throw them coins in
order to be 'spared'*

I Like to Stay Up

I like to stay up
and listen
when big people talking
jumbie stories

I does feel
so tingly and excited
inside me

But when my mother say
"Girl, time for bed"

Then is when
I does feel a dread

Then is when
I does jump into me bed

Then is when
I does cover up
from me feet to me head

Then is when
I does wish I didn't listen
to no stupid jumbie story

Then is when
I does wish I did read
me book instead

Grace Nichols

Jumbie: A Guyanese word for ghost

Advice to a Young Ghost

"Please remember,
Whatever you do
Don't spook until
You're spooken to."

Trevor Harvey

PLUCKER OF MOONBEAMS

A Hallowe'en Charm For Sweet Dreams

May the ghost
  lie in its grave.
May the vampire
  see the light.
May the witch
  keep to her cave.
And the spectre
  melt from sight.

May the wraith
  stay in the wood.
May the banshee
  give no fright.
May the ghoul
  be gone for good.
And the zombie
  haste in flight.

May the troll
  no more be seen.
May the werewolf
  lose its bite.
May all the spooks
  and children green
Fade forever

  in

   the

    night...

Wes Magee

Owl

"Owl
Who?
Who are you?
Who?"

    "I am owl,
    night's eyes,
    wise beyond understanding."

"Who?
Who are you?
Who?"

    "I am owl,
    shadow of shadows,
    owner of forests,
    beautiful beyond comprehension."

"Who?
Who are you?
Who?"

    "I am owl,
    plucker of moonbeams;
    owl, most mysterious.
    Beware."

Patricia Hubbell

Counting Horrors

1 witch with 1 broomstick,
1 tooth and 1 cat,
1 cauldron, 1 spider:
how many is that?   [ ]

2 fangs and 1 dracula,
speared by 1 stake,
8 victims around him:
now what does that make?   [ ]

9 ghosts scare 12 people
in dark stormy weather,
then hide in 3 castles:
what's that altogether?   [ ]

1 monster with 10 legs,
8 toes (not a lot),
20 eyes and 9 heads:
add them up – it makes what?   [ ]

When you've found the four numbers,
write down and then see
what you think the next number
in line ought to be.   [ ]

Charles Thomson

Windy Nights

Whenever the moon and stars are set,
    Whenever the wind is high,
All night long in the dark and wet,
    A man goes riding by.
Late in the night when the fires are out,
Why does he gallop and gallop about?

Whenever the trees are crying aloud,
    And ships are tossed at sea,
By, on the highway, low and loud,
    By at the gallop goes he:
By at the gallop he goes, and then
By he comes back at the gallop again.

Robert Louis Stevenson

LAST WORD

Song of Two Ghosts

My friend
This is a wide world
We're travelling over
Walking on the moonlight.

American Indian song from
Omaha, North America

Acknowledgements

The publishers gratefully acknowledge permission to reproduce the following copyright material:

Moira Andrew for the use of 'House for Sale', 'Holiday Home' and 'Just Pretending' from *The Unsaid Goodnight* by Phil Carradice. © 1989, Moira Andrew (1989, Stride Publications).

Andrew Mann Literary Agency and Random House Children's Books for the use of 'Gobbledespook' from *Picture a Poem* by Gina Douthwaite. © 1994, Gina Douthwaite (1994, Hutchinson Children's Books).

Clare Bevan for the use of 'The New Girl'.

Bloomsbury Publishing for the use of 'The Longest Journey in the World' from *Mustard, Custard, Grumble Belly and Gravy* by Michael Rosen. © 2007, Michael Rosen (2007, Bloomsbury).

Caroline Sheldon Literary Agency for the use of 'Duppy Dan' from *Under the Moon and Over the Sea* by John Agard. © 2002, John Agard (2002, Walker Books).

Xanna Eve Chown for the use of 'Scaredy Bat'.

Paul Cookson for the use of 'The Haunted Poem'.

Graeme Curry for the use of 'Midnight in the Chip Shop'.

Jennifer Curry for the use of 'Weighty Problem', and 'A School Girl Called Julia' and 'A Shy Ghost Called Freddy' by Jenny Craig.

Curtis Brown Group Ltd, London for the use of 'I Like to Stay Up' from *Come on into My Tropical Garden* by Grace Nichols. © 1988, Grace Nichols (1988, A&C Black).

David Higham Associates for the use of 'Morning Monster' and 'Terrible Toast' by Tony Mitton, 'Green Man in the Garden' from *Collected Poems for Children* by Charles Causley, © 1996, Charles Causley (1996, Macmillan), and 'Quieter Than Snow', 'Trees' and 'Ghost in the Garden' from

Walking on Air by Berlie Doherty, © 1999, Berlie Doherty (2014, KDP).

Jan Dean for the use of 'The Jelly Bone Man'.

Peter Dixon for the use of 'Sam Spook'.

Eddison Pearson for the use of 'Duppy Jamboree' from *Duppy Jamboree* by Valerie Bloom. © 1992, Valerie Bloom (1992, Cambridge University Press).

Sheilagh Finney for the use of 'It' by Eric Finney.

David Harmer for the use of 'Watch Your Teacher Carefully'.

HarperCollins Publishers (USA) for the use of 'Skeleton Parade' from *It's Halloween* by Jack Prelutsky. © 2001, Jack Prelutsky (2001, Turtleback Books).

Trevor Harvey for the use of 'Advice to a Young Ghost'.

Ivan Jones for the use of 'Vanilla Van Ghost'.

Ian Larmont for the use of 'Old Bill Bones'.

Laura Cecil Literary Agency for the use of 'The Two Old Women of Mumbling Hill' by James Reeves. © James Reeves.

Patricia Leighton for the use of 'Invite to Cool Ghouls'.

Wes Magee for the use of 'In the Castle of Gloom' and 'A Hallowe'en Charm for Sweet Dreams'.

Marian Reiner Literary Agency for the use of 'Teeny Tiny Ghost' by Lilian Moore, © 1972, Lilian Moore (all rights renewed and reserved), and 'Owl' by Patricia Hubbell from *Catch Me a Wind*, © 1968, Patricia Hubble (1968, Atheneum).

Robin Mellor for the use of 'The Ghost Outside' and 'The Gribble'.

John Mole for the use of 'Riddle' from *Once There Were Dragons* by John Mole. © 1979, John Mole (1979, Deutsch).

Brian Moses for the use of 'The Ghoul School Bus'.

Judith Nicholls for the use of 'Ghost Child' and 'Deserted House'.

David Orme for the use of 'I'd Rather Not Tell'.

Penguin Books Australia for the use of 'Disbelief' from *In the Garden of Bad Things* by Doug MacLeod. © 1982, Doug MacLeod (1982, Viking).

Peters Fraser & Dunlop for the use of 'The Longest Journey in the World' from *You Can't Catch Me* by Michael Rosen. © 2003, Michael Rosen (2003, Andre Deutsch).

David Poulter for the use of 'Beware'.

John Rice for the use of 'Ghost Hunt'.

Daphne Schiller for the use of 'Hallowe'en'.

The Society of Authors for the use of 'Someone' by Walter de la Mare.

Charles Thomson for the use of 'Counting Horrors'.

Nick Toczek for the use of 'Scary Night'.

Jill Townsend for the use of 'Do Not Feed' from *Hubble Bubble* by Andrew Fusek Peters. © 2003, Jill Townsend (2003, Hodder Wayland).

Linda Lee Welch for the use of 'Night Water'.

Kit Wright for the use of 'Ghosts' from *Rabbiting On* by Kit Wright. © 1986, Kit Wright (1986, HarperCollins).

Every effort has been made to trace copyright holders for the works reproduced in this book, and the publishers apologise for any inadvertent omissions.